GRIMM

Original stories by the Brothers Grimm
Retold by Jan Davidson
Series Advisor Professor Kimberley Reynolds
Illustrated by Niroot Puttapipat

OXFORD
UNIVERSITY PRESS

Letter from the Author

I was a late reader, taught by my
mother. Once I could read on
my own, I never stopped, reading
anything I could lay my hands on
at home, in the school library and
my local bookshop. I was always
reading under the blankets with
a torch, having been caught with
a book way after my bedtime! It
didn't stop me visiting all those other worlds from
the safety and comfort of my own bed.

I chose the Brothers Grimm's fairy tales
because they were amongst my favourites as a
child. I studied English at Oxford, then worked in
publishing before having my three children.
I have written short stories, poetry and a novel
and I also have an unusual day job, working in
a Cambridge college, researching and writing
obituaries: the real stories of people's lives.

Jan Davidson

Little Brother and Little Sister

One day a little brother took his little sister by the hand and said, 'Sis, let's run away together. There's nothing left for us here. Since our mother died, you know as well as I do that our lives have been made a total misery by our wicked stepmother. She never misses an opportunity to belittle us and abuse us. She has never shown us any love. In fact, I cannot remember a moment's happiness since she came into our home. Even the dog is treated better than us, fed juicy chunks of meat off the table whilst we are left to starve. If our mother was still alive, she would be horrified by the deliberate cruelty of that woman. She feels nothing for us and would prefer it if we did not exist at all! Have you seen the way she looks at us sometimes with those yellow eyes? It is as if they are burning right through you. It wouldn't surprise me to find out she is a witch!' The boy laughed, both of the children shivering involuntarily at the thought.

'You are right,' his little sister agreed. 'Let's run away together and make our own lives in a place far away from here.'

As evening sun dappled the hills with its golden light the pair set off, walking in no particular direction, until they came to a dark wood. The shadows were beginning to loom large and the children were now cold and hungry. They were afraid, too. The night was alive with strange sounds and they both trembled and clung to one another for comfort. Eventually, they stumbled across a large tree with a hollowed-out trunk. Shivering, they crawled inside and lay on a bed of dried leaves and bracken, convinced they would perish from the cold. But the tree's thick trunk protected them from the frost, and in the morning the sun's rays warmed its bark.

When the children awoke, Little Brother was extremely thirsty. 'Let's see if we can find a river or a stream,' he suggested.

'What use is water to us when we are starving, dear brother?' sobbed his sister. 'We are surely going to die of starvation!' Then she threw herself down on her leaf bed and cried until she ran out of tears. The little brother was distraught at seeing his sister's misery. But wisely he said nothing. Instead, he quietly took her by the hand. 'Come with me, Little Sister,' he coaxed. He pulled her to her feet, and she followed him back out of the hollow into the dazzling morning.

Meanwhile, their wicked stepmother had discovered the children had vanished. When she saw how they were living in the forest, her fury knew no bounds and she was determined to have her revenge. How dare they try to outwit her by running away? She set a cunning trap to thwart their happiness. Conjuring up a stream near the children's resting place, she knew its happy gurgling would entice the children to go and drink from its crystal-clear waters. But there was a nasty surprise lurking in those waters. Whoever drank from the spring would be turned into a fawn.

The children heard the murmuring stream and their mouths watered in anticipation of quenching their thirst in its sparkling shallows. How it glistened and sang in the sunlight! Little Brother crouched down and bent his head down close to its surface, so great was his desire to drink the water.

Little Sister, who had been sitting as still as a statue at the water's edge, had been listening intently to the stream. Now her expression turned from delight to one of horror. She had heard the stream murmuring its warning: 'Beware! Whoever drinks from me will be turned into a fawn! Whoever drinks from me will be turned into a fawn!' Terrified, the girl begged her brother not to touch the water with his lips. But her pleading fell on deaf ears.

'Don't be ridiculous!' replied her brother. 'All I can hear is the bubbling of the stream as it flows over the

rocks. There is really nothing to fear. Just watch me!' he cried, cupping his hands and leaning down to take his first sip. But no sooner had the first translucent drop touched his lips, he was transformed into a fawn.

How the girl wept when she saw what had befallen her brother. Inconsolable, she set about gathering the bulrushes that grew at the water's edge and wove a rope to tether and lead the fawn. She did not want to risk losing her dear brother, now he was transformed into an animal.

Now the wicked stepmother was incandescent with rage when she saw only one of the children had succumbed to her spell. The girl was still free, but she would see to it she suffered, too. It was just a matter of time. The wicked stepmother waited for her next opportunity to inflict harm.

The little sister set about making the best of their altered circumstances. She led the little fawn through the forest until they came to a cave. Here she made their home, collecting velvety green moss to make a soft bed for the two to share, Little Sister sleeping with her head propped against the silky belly of the fawn. In this way they comforted one another.

All through the night Little Sister felt the warm pulse of his beating heart. At least there was still another living presence to soften the pain of her loneliness! It gave her solace even though she missed her brother's human form more than anything.

Each morning, she would take him to the meadow where the emerald grass grew in lush abundance. She took pleasure in watching him gambol and munch to his heart's content. Even the wild animals treated the pair with kindness when they witnessed the way in which the little sister cared for the fawn.

In this way they lived for many years in happy obscurity, until the little sister had grown into a young woman and the fawn into a fine stag.

However, one day their fortunes changed. A king came riding through the forest nearby and became separated from his men. Completely lost, he chanced upon a clearing where the girl was walking with the stag, golden shafts of sunlight dappling the pair of them as they moved together through the glade. The King was stopped in his tracks, so stunned was he by the beauty of the scene and the girl in particular. He immediately galloped after them, scooping the girl up onto his horse. Then he tethered the stag by its horns to his saddle and rode back to the palace.

Now the lives of the brother and sister were changed beyond all recognition. The King and Queen made them most welcome. The girl was waited on and treated as if she were indeed of royal blood. She kept the stag close to her at all times, feeding him delicacies from her gold plate and letting him drink water from her silver goblet.

Sadly, the young Queen became ill and died before her time and the King was extremely sad. He found the little sister a great solace to him during the dark months that followed his bereavement. It was therefore no surprise when the King married the little sister and made her his new Queen. This was a cause for great rejoicing, since she was already loved by all who knew her.

However, it was not long before the wicked stepmother heard rumours of the marriage between the King and the girl with the stag, and immediately she realized it must be the little sister. She had hoped the girl had perished in the forest, torn to pieces by wild animals or starved to death. The wicked stepmother was very angry at having failed to lure the girl into her trap. To discover she was now a queen ... this was an outrage! She became obsessed with the idea of revenge, her every hour devoted to plotting and planning the poor girl's downfall.

It came to pass that the Queen became pregnant and the King was overjoyed at the prospect of becoming a father. Unfortunately for the Queen, the King was away hunting when she gave birth to their beautiful baby boy.

All the bells rang throughout the land in celebration of this momentous occasion. The wicked stepmother, deep in the forest, heard them ring and her heart turned black with malice. This was the moment she had been waiting for and she seized it with relish. Disguising herself as a nurse, she managed to talk her way past the guards and into the palace until she eventually came to the Queen's bedchamber.

There the poor Queen lay, frail and exhausted in
her bed, her flawless complexion as white as alabaster.
When she saw a nurse had been sent to her, she was only
too grateful for her assistance.

'Shall I run you a bath?' enquired the nurse in her
sweetest voice. 'The warm water will relax you and do
you good after such a long birth.'

The Queen, who was so innocent and trusting, did
not suspect her at all. Placing her new baby in his crib,
she slowly raised herself from her bed and allowed the
nurse to help her across the room.

'I have filled a lovely warm bath to the brim,' the nurse murmured encouragingly as she pushed the Queen through the bathroom door, slammed it shut and locked it behind her. Now the poor Queen found herself in a room full of hot coals. She screamed and banged on the door. But nobody heard her frantic cries for help as the steam enveloped her. There were no windows and the room was small. The glowing coals burned with such intensity the Queen soon lost consciousness and died, suffocated by the heat.

Now the wicked stepmother happened to have a daughter of her own who she prized greatly. This was her chance to usurp the King. Using her supernatural powers, she transformed her daughter into an exact replica of

the dead Queen and instructed her to climb into the bed. It appeared as if nothing had changed.

When the King returned, triumphant from his hunting trip, he was overjoyed to find the Queen had given birth to their first child. He was so delighted with and preoccupied by his young son, he did not detect any change in his wife. However, one of the chambermaids had noticed how the Queen had changed, showing little affection towards her baby in recent days and displaying an icy disdain when speaking to her servants. Gone was the warmth and affection they had all grown to expect from their Queen. But there was another reason for the chambermaid's suspicion that all was not as it appeared.

It was her habit to sit between the Queen's bed and the crib containing the baby prince. In this manner, she could transfer the baby swiftly if he needed to be fed by his mother. One night she was seated as usual, drifting between wakefulness and sleep, waiting for the young prince to wake for his feed. She was aware the Queen still lay in her bed, the mouth set in a hard, unnatural line even in sleep. Indeed, she could discern the rise and fall of her bedclothes in time to her snoring. (This was unlike the Queen, for she never used to snore at all!)

However, suddenly the room was flooded with moonlight and there before her stood another Queen, both strange and yet more familiar, a soft smile playing about her lips.

The chambermaid watched as she glided across to the crib where the young prince lay happily gurgling and playing with his fingers. Picking him up, she put him to her breast, rocking him gently and singing him a lullaby as she fed him in the darkness. Then she carefully laid him back in his crib, lovingly rearranging his bedding.

Floating over to where the stag lay on his side, twitching in his sleep, she crouched down and slowly stroked the soft sheen of his hide. Then with a heavy sigh, she rose to her feet and disappeared. Although how she disappeared, the chambermaid could only guess. The door of the bedchamber was shut fast. Indeed, it was almost as if she evaporated into thin air. The ghostly vision the chambermaid had just witnessed was a phantom, she was sure, and yet it was more real than the Queen who lay in the royal bed.

15

But on the following night, when the room was blanched white by the moon, the chambermaid saw something else. The Queen, having fed and settled the young prince, moved across to the stag. Again, she stroked his soft hide with such tenderness it brought tears to the woman's eyes. Then the chambermaid was astonished as the Queen opened her lips and spoke to the animal, asking:

'How is my baby and my fawn?

I'll come twice more

And then I'm gone!'

Then she rose and turned, a beautiful apparition, and dissolved into the shadows. The chambermaid did not know whether she was awake or dreaming. However she waited until morning and then she went directly to the King and described what she had witnessed in the night. He listened carefully to her description of the Queen and he was as bewildered as the maid.

The King was now curious, too. The following night, he crept from the bed he shared with the Queen and concealed himself behind a large velvet curtain and waited to see what transpired. He did not have to wait long. At the same hour as the previous

16

night, an ethereal image of his lovely wife appeared in the bedchamber, whilst in the royal bed he was shocked to see how the figure of his supposed wife stirred slightly and snorted in her sleep.

Meanwhile, he observed how the ghostly Queen glided over to the cradle, scooped her son into her arms, and fed him with great tenderness. Rocking him gently in her arms, she sang to the baby prince in such sweet tones. It was like a fountain overflowing. The tears sprang to his eyes, for he had not heard such sweetness in her voice for some time. Indeed, now he came to think of it, his wife had appeared rather cold and distant in recent days. But now the sound was enough to melt even the hardest heart!

Swaddling the little prince in his blanket, she sighed heavily as she laid him back in his crib. Turning away, she floated across the room to where the fawn slept on a velvet cushion and began to stroke him, speaking in the soft low voice the King knew so well:

'How is my baby and my fawn?

I'll come once more

And then I am gone!'

The King was in such agonies when he heard her voice, he had to control his impulse to jump out from behind the curtain and embrace her, so great was his longing at that moment. How could he have ever been deceived by the pale imitation of his wife who lay next to him in bed? Now he knew she was an imposter and he longed for the wife he had lost. He yearned to take her in his arms because he knew in his heart of hearts this fleeting vision was the true image of his wife.

The King resolved to see if she returned for a fourth time. The following night he watched and waited, and again witnessed the Queen come into the room and care for her baby and the fawn. The King held his breath as she glided from one to the other, stroking the animal and asking:

'How is my baby and my fawn?

I'll come no more

And then I am gone.'

But on this occasion, all caution deserted the King. He had to tell her he loved her. He ran to the Queen and took her in his arms. Then something extraordinary happened; instantly, the Queen's ghostly image was transformed back into a flesh and blood woman. The wicked stepmother's spell was broken! The King was astonished and delighted to find his wife restored to him in all her living, breathing beauty. The wicked stepmother's treachery revealed, he now realized the woman he had treated as his Queen and his wife was a traitor.

The King decreed the wicked stepmother and her daughter should be severely punished for their deception. He wanted them to suffer the same deprivations as Little Brother and Little Sister. Therefore, the pair were taken deep into the forest where they were forced to forage and live amongst the wild animals. They lived in constant fear of being attacked because no creature loved them.

One day they came to the enchanted stream and before the wicked stepmother could shout a warning, her daughter had stooped to drink its crystal waters. She was immediately turned into a fawn and took fright and fled. But the wicked stepmother, howling with rage and despair, toppled into the stream only to be immediately turned to stone.

At that very moment, far away at the palace, the stag was transformed back into his human form. Now he was a tall handsome young man and the Queen was overjoyed to be finally reunited with her brother. At last her joy was complete and they all lived together happily until the end of their days on this earth.

21

The Goose Girl

There was once a queen who had an only child: a beautiful princess who was the apple of her eye and the rose of her heart. The Queen was a widow and she loved her daughter more than anything in the world. However, the day came when the princess was betrothed to marry a prince who lived in a distant kingdom. With a heavy heart, the Queen collected together a dowry made up of gold, silver, precious jewellery and fine goblets. She gave them to the princess to take with her to her new life. The Queen then went to her bedchamber where she pricked her finger with a knife and allowed three ruby drops of blood to fall onto her white handkerchief. She gave the handkerchief to her daughter, telling her to keep it with her at all times because it had the power to protect her from harm.

Finally, the Queen gave the princess a chambermaid as her servant. The chambermaid was hardly delighted at the prospect of serving the princess because she happened to loathe her with a vengeance. She resented her for both her beauty and her royal status, and wanted nothing more than to teach her a lesson.

'Why should she, by some accident of birth, be the one who has all the airs and graces and the fancy dresses?' the chambermaid grumbled to herself. 'I am just as good as her, if not better. Why did Fate decree she should be a princess and I a lowly chambermaid? We'll see about that!'

The Queen had also given the princess two horses for their journey. The princess's horse was called Falada and was unique in that it was able to speak.

With a heavy heart, the princess bade her mother farewell and began her long journey. The day grew hot as they rode. The sun blazed in a still blue sky, and flowers hung their heads limply in the sweltering heat.

'Let us stop here to rest,' suggested the princess when they reached a burbling brook, its crystal waters dancing in the shade. The princess's parched mouth was as dry as dust. 'How thirsty I am!' she declared. 'Please fetch me some water in a goblet,' she commanded the chambermaid.

'Fetch it yourself!' the chambermaid snapped. 'I do not like being a servant and I have no intention of being yours!'

More than a little perplexed by her rudeness, the princess dismounted. She was a sensitive girl and would not intentionally have hurt a fly. Perhaps she had been too abrupt in her manner, she reflected. After all, should she not treat everyone with equal respect? Perhaps the chambermaid was right after all. Yes, even as a princess, she should practise the art of humility, she decided. Indeed, she was not too proud to kneel down by the brook and cup her hands to drink its water until her thirst was quenched.

But the handkerchief, a loyal servant of the Queen, felt obliged to comment on the scene it had just witnessed, saying, 'If your mother only knew, her heart would break in two!'

The princess and the chambermaid resumed their journey as the sun climbed higher and higher and heat rippled in waves from the ground. Not a single leaf stirred on the trees. Even the birds had stopped singing. All life was suspended in the shimmering heat.

The pair had reached the bend of a fast-flowing river. Again, driven by her insatiable thirst the princess asked to stop.

'Please will you fetch me some water from the river in one of those goblets?' she politely asked the chambermaid.

'I have told you once and I'll tell you again – I am no servant of yours!' snapped the girl. 'If you are so thirsty, fetch it yourself.'

Sighing, the princess jumped down from her horse for a second time and knelt down on the cool green bank of the river to drink from her hands. She was not too proud to satisfy her thirst in this way.

But the handkerchief, mortified on her behalf, spoke again. 'If only your mother knew, her heart would break in two!'

They continued on their way. But when the princess reached in her pocket for the handkerchief it was empty. The princess gasped with horror. She must have dropped it in the river as she stooped to drink. Now she was on her own!

The chambermaid, observing the reason for her distress, was delighted. She realised, with some satisfaction, the princess no longer had the protection of the magic powers of the handkerchief. Since they were almost at their journey's end, she knew she must act swiftly.

'Get down from your horse,' she ordered the princess. 'Take off that fine dress!'

The princess was so shocked by the threatening manner of the chambermaid, she did not dare refuse. Indeed, she was such a gentle soul, for a brief moment she almost felt she must deserve such punishment for having unwittingly caused the girl some great offence. Quivering, the princess dismounted and did as she was told.

One by one, everything slipped to the ground. The silk cloak edged with furs and the fine embroidered dress. The chambermaid scooped it all up and hastily attired herself in the clothes of her mistress. In a callous reversal of fortune, she made the princess put on her plain clothes and take her old nag to ride instead. Triumphant, the chambermaid leaped onto Falada's back and galloped ahead towards the palace, the old nag trailing behind.

The King and his son were already waiting in the grand courtyard of the palace. On her arrival, the chambermaid was treated with the respect reserved for the royal bride and taken to a sumptuous feast to celebrate her wedding to the prince. But the King, who was an observant man, was struck by the refinement and beauty of the girl accompanying the chambermaid.

'Who is she?' he enquired that evening as the celebrations continued. He watched as the girl served gold platters piled with delicacies, her eyes glittering with tears like sapphires in the darkness.

'Oh, she is nothing but a lowly servant girl I picked up along the way to keep me company,' snorted the false bride, waving her hand dismissively. 'Can't you find her something useful to do?'

She was eager to have the princess out of the way in order to protect her own position at court. The King stroked his silver beard and thought long and hard. He had few suitable opportunities for another servant. Then he had a flash of inspiration. She could help tend the geese!

So the real princess was sent to tend to his geese with Conrad, the goose boy.

But still the false bride was worried her own treachery might be discovered. She feared the princess's loyal horse, Falada, might open his mouth and tell the truth about her treachery.

With a black heart she went to her husband. 'You know that horse I rode here on?' she began, coyly. 'He nearly threw me off his back on a number of occasions. Please can you arrange for the knacker to take him away and cut his head off, to be sure he is dead?'

The prince did as she asked and ordered the knacker to kill Falada.

When the real princess heard of Falada's cruel fate, she wept as if the world had ended. In desperation, she went to visit the knacker in his yard.

'Please,' she begged him, 'when you cut off Falada's head, will you do this one thing for me? Take his head and nail it above the main archway in the city wall so each morning and evening I can see him as I drive the geese. In return I will give you this gold coin,' she offered.

The knacker, who was moved more by the quiet dignity of the goose girl and less by the reward, agreed to her request. He did as he was bade and hung the dead horse's head where the princess could see it as she passed beneath the arch each day.

The following day, the princess rose at dawn and went with Conrad the goose boy to drive the geese out of the city gates to the meadow. This morning as she looked up, she saw Falada's head hammered to the arch, just as the knacker had promised. The princess, moved to tears, lamented, 'Oh my poor Falada.'

Then the head answered her.

'Dear princess, is that really you?
Oh, if only your mother knew,
The fate of one so fair and true,
Her very heart would break in two!'

The princess continued on her way in silence,

so stricken with grief was she at the loss of her horse.
When she reached the meadow, she sat down amongst
the sweet-smelling flowers and loosened her long
golden hair so that it floated freely in the breeze.
Slowly she began to brush it. Conrad, idly watching
the princess, was entranced at the sight of her hair. It
reminded him of ripe corn, its texture that of the finest
silk, as it floated about her. If only he could touch it
and keep some of it! Conrad playfully lunged at her
and tried to pluck a few strands. But the princess would
have none of it and cried:

'Blow, wind, blow with all your might!
Blow Conrad's cap out of sight,
Make him chase it everywhere,
Until I've braided all my hair
And fixed it so it's held so tight.'

The wind suddenly whipped up into a fury and blew Conrad's cap off his head so that it flew like a bird away across the fields, with Conrad in hot pursuit.

By the time he had retrieved it and slapped it back on his head, the princess had finished brushing her hair and had tightly re-braided it. Not a single strand remained loose. Conrad, furious at being thwarted, would not speak to the princess for the rest of the day. As the sun slipped behind the palace, the goose girl and Conrad ushered the geese back into the city.

The next morning, the princess and Conrad rose with the birds in a lilac dawn and drove the geese out of the city through the arch where Falada's head had been hammered up. Again, the sight of him stopped the princess in her tracks and she said, 'Oh my poor Falada.'

And Falada responded:

'Dear princess, is that really you?
Oh, if only your mother knew,
The fate of one so fair and true,
Her very heart would break in two!'

She continued on her way to the meadow and sat down in the damp morning dew that hung in pearls about her. Again, she let loose her hair as the first rays of sun gilded the earth. Conrad watched, enchanted, as her hair unwound about her in clouds of gold. He just had to possess a few of those tantalising strands! Again, he tried to grab a handful. But the princess was too quick for him. She shouted:

'Blow, wind, blow with all your might!
Blow Conrad's cap out of sight,
And make him chase it everywhere
Until I've braided all my hair
And fixed it so it's held so tight.'

Immediately the wind blustered and blew so hard, Conrad's cap flew skywards as the boy jumped up and chased it across the meadow and over the brow of the hill. The goose girl laughed as she plaited her hair and pinned it up again. By the time Conrad reappeared, his cheeks red as he puffed and panted with rage, not a strand remained untamed.

They continued to tend the geese until evening fell and they returned to the palace. But this time, Conrad had had enough of being teased. He went direct to the King and complained bitterly about the goose girl. He told the King he no longer wished to work with her.

The King was curious and when he asked him why, Conrad replied, 'Each morning as we pass through the archway that leads out of the city, the goose girl stops to speak to a horse's head attached to the wall. She always says the same thing: "Oh, poor Falada, I see you hanging there." And the head answers her:

"Dear princess, is that really you?
Oh, if your mother only knew,
The fate of one so fair and true
Her very heart would break in two!"'

He also told the King how when they were in the meadow he tried to pluck a few hairs from her golden head and how, in retaliation, she had whipped up a wind and sent him running after his cap. All he wanted was a few strands of that golden hair.

Although Conrad was not amused, the King could not help the smile spreading beneath his silver beard. Intrigued by the strange behaviour of the goose girl, the King was also moved by the description of her exchanges with Falada, so he decided to investigate Conrad's story for himself.

Having instructed the boy to accompany the girl to the meadow as usual the next morning, the King disguised himself by wearing a large cloak and hat and hid in the gloom of the archway. From his secret place, he observed what happened next.

He waited until the goose girl came past, driving the geese in a flurry of quacks and feathers. When she saw Falada, she stopped dead in her tracks and tilted her tear-stained face upwards to speak to the poor horse. Indeed, the scene he witnessed between the goose girl and Falada was enough to soften the heart of the hardest king. He then followed her at a distance until she reached the lush meadow where she sat amidst the flowers and let down her hair, the colour of buttercups.

He observed the boy try to creep up on her, his hand outstretched to catch the golden strands. But the goose girl, who had spied him out of the corner of her eye, called:

'Blow, wind, blow with all your might!
Blow Conrad's cap out of sight,
And make him chase it everywhere
Until I've braided all my hair
And fixed it so it's held so tight.'

Then the wind snatched the cap off his head and Conrad was away, chasing after it, chasing over hill and vale. By the time he reappeared, red in the face, the goose girl had already rearranged her hair in coiling plaits about her head. The King was amused by what he saw, but he was also intrigued. So that evening when the goose girl returned to the palace, he called her before him.

'Tell me,' he said, 'why is it you do these strange things?'

When the King quizzed her, the poor girl turned the colour of milk and began to quake in her boots.

'Believe me, Your Majesty, I would tell you if I could,' she trembled. 'But I have sworn to the heavenly skies not to complain about my fate and to keep my secret safe within my breast. If I had not sworn, I feared for my very life!' (The chambermaid had continued to threaten her, boasting she had the ear of the King and the prince and all she had to do was click her fingers and the princess would be executed, just like Falada!)

The King tried to make the girl to divulge her secret to him. But as much as he pressed her, she remained as immoveable as the palace itself. No amount of persuasion would make her break her vow.

'It is more than my life is worth,' she told him sadly.

'Well, if you won't tell me your secret, perhaps there is another way,' the King replied. He remembered there was a large stove in the palace kitchen that was no longer in use. He bade the princess follow him there and showed her the stove. 'Why don't you climb inside and confess your secret to the stove?' he suggested. 'There, you will be safe from prying ears and your vow will not be broken,' he reassured her.

The princess, anxious to unburden herself, willingly climbed into the dark belly of the stove. Crouching in the velvet blackness, she revealed everything to it, her gentle voice echoing around the chamber. Little did she suspect the King had positioned himself at the chimney and was quietly listening to every word.

'Here I am, lonely and forsaken by the entire world,' sighed the goose girl. 'Forced by my maidservant to exchange clothes so she could trick the prince into a false marriage. And now I am a mere goose girl who spends her life in the meadow with Conrad chasing my golden hair. Not only did I lose the magic handkerchief, my beloved horse Falada has been taken from me and killed. Oh, if my mother knew, her heart would indeed break in two!'

Then the princess wept as if the world had ended and her heart would never mend. But now the King knew her secret and when she emerged from the black stove, he was waiting for her.

'Dear child, I heard every word,' he told her. The goose girl shook with fear, but the King smiled and said, 'Your suffering is now at an end.'

He called at once for his servants and had the goose girl taken to the royal apartments where she was bathed and dressed in fine robes worthy of a princess. Once again, the King marvelled at her refinement and her beauty. Now he wished to restore her to her rightful place.

The King then summoned his son to him and explained how he had been deceived into marrying the chambermaid. He recounted how the real princess had been sent to work as a goose girl at the palace. This she had done with humility and without complaint, he added. Therefore, when the prince was introduced to his real bride, he was impressed both by her virtue and her beauty. At last he had found his true mate!

The King and the prince decreed there should be a huge banquet to which all their friends and courtiers were invited to celebrate the occasion. It was arranged so that the prince was seated at the head of the banqueting table and on one side sat the chambermaid, whilst on the other was seated the real princess.

The chambermaid, who was so dazzled and distracted by the occasion, failed to recognize her former mistress in all her shimmering finery. The chambermaid was gullible indeed!

After all the feasting and drinking, the King decided to put the chambermaid to the test by posing a riddle for her to solve.

'If a woman deceives her lord, what punishment does she deserve?' he asked, all the time observing her closely.

The false bride merrily walked straight into the trap he had set for her. 'Why, if she plays false with her lord, she should be punished severely,' she blithely answered. 'I would have her shoved inside a wooden barrel lined with the sharpest nails. Two white horses would then be harnessed to the barrel and forced to drag it through the streets.'

There were gasps from some of the courtiers as the King rose from the banqueting table, his face like a thundercloud, his finger pointed at the chambermaid.

'You are that woman!' he grimly declared. 'Therefore, you have pronounced your own sentence! This is exactly what will happen to you!'

The chambermaid gasped and shook her fist at the real princess as she let out an anguished cry and jumped on a chair to try to evade capture. But she was immediately arrested by the King's guards and dragged out of the palace, kicking and cursing. She was then placed inside a barrel and pulled around the palace grounds, then out along the bumpy cobbled streets, then beneath the arch where Falada's head was still fixed, his sad eyes following her, hurtling onwards to her death.

Now the King was delighted his son had now been reunited with his real bride, a girl he considered worthy of his son. For the King had seen in her something truly remarkable. Whether as a princess or a lowly goose girl, she had shown herself to be true to herself and to others. She had acted with humility and kindness, despite her ordeal. It was therefore with great joy they celebrated their marriage and reigned over their kingdom together for many years afterwards, in peace, harmony and happiness.

The Water of Life

There was once a king who fell seriously ill and it was thought he might die. Gloomily, his courtiers began to make plans for a grand state funeral.

The King had three sons and they met in the palace gardens to discuss events and prepare for the worst. However, it was only the youngest son who felt any real love for their father. The older two, preferring to put their own needs first, immediately started an argument over who might inherit the kingdom and all its assets once their father was dead and buried. It was left to the youngest son to try to intervene, reminding them the King was not dead yet. Indeed, he dared to suggest there might still be time to save the King.

Whilst they were discussing their father and squabbling over the bleak turn of events, an old man happened to be strolling past them. When he saw the sorry scene, he paused to ask them the source of their misery. They explained their father was gravely ill, with little hope of survival, and how they had tried everything in an attempt to save him.

The best physicians had examined the King and had shaken their heads and gone away again, unable to form a diagnosis of his symptoms. They had declared him beyond help and left the princes without hope.

The old man listened intently to their story. Then he smiled a slow crinkled smile and said, 'Do not despair, young princes, for I have heard of a cure. It is called the Water of Life. If the King drinks this, he will regain his health. However, it is extremely hard to find the source of the water.'

'Well I shall find it!' declared the oldest of the three brothers, leaping to his feet. He immediately went to the King who lay in his vast bed, a pale shadow of his former self. When he told his father he wished to embark on a quest for the Water of Life, the King's hands trembled as he clutched the arm of his firstborn.

'No!' he gasped. 'I cannot let you go and risk your life for mine; the danger is too great.'

But the prince was very persistent and eventually the King relented and agreed to his request, albeit with a heavy heart.

However the prince's motives were not entirely altruistic. He saw this as his chance to prove himself to his father. If he returned with the water, he would naturally be the apple of his father's eye and inherit the entire kingdom on his death. (He had always felt somewhat eclipsed by his siblings.)

The prince then bade his father farewell, saddled up his horse, and rode away into the wilderness in search of the Water of Life. After he had been riding for some days, he was accosted by a dwarf who leaped out of the bushes in front of him and enquired, 'Where are you going in such haste?'

'Get out of my way, you fool!' shouted the prince. 'It's none of your business.'

The dwarf was furious at being treated with such contempt and as the prince cantered away, he put a spell on him. The prince continued his journey and thought nothing more of the incident. He eventually entered a mountain gorge, its steep sides allowing just a small chink of light to illuminate his path. But as he rode, the sides moved closer and closer together until it became impassable and he was wedged between the rocks. Struggle as he might, he was completely trapped, still sitting astride his fine horse.

Meanwhile, the King had waited patiently for his son to return bearing the cure. But as hours turned into days his optimism faded and he grew steadily weaker.

The second son, seeing his father's grave state, stepped forward. 'Father,' he said, 'it is possible my brother is dead, so let me go search for the Water of Life.'

Secretly, he too hoped to ingratiate himself in his father's affections so he might inherit everything when the King died.

The King, having lost one son, was none too happy about allowing another to follow in his footsteps. But the prince was so persuasive and the King was indeed a desperate man so eventually he relented and agreed to the request.

The prince departed at breakneck speed and cantered off along the same road taken by his older brother. However it was not long before he too was stopped in his tracks by the dwarf and asked where he was going in such haste.

'Get out of my way you fool, it's none of your business!' retorted the prince, his manner one of extreme arrogance. He pulled hard on the reins, his horse rearing and threatening to crush the dwarf beneath its flailing hooves. Then he galloped off in a cloud of dust. The dwarf, outraged the prince's conceited behaviour, placed the same curse on him.

Just like his brother, the prince rode into the gorge and found himself imprisoned by the rocks on either side with no means of escape.

Again the King waited in vain for his second son to return. Finally, the youngest prince could bear it no longer, so he went to his father and begged for permission to go and find his brothers and bring back the Water of Life.

Unlike the other two, his motives came from a pure heart. He loved the old King and could not bear the thought of losing him. The King was stricken at the thought of losing his beloved son. But the boy was very persuasive and with great reluctance the King allowed him to set forth on his quest.

The prince set off along the same highway as his brothers and the same dwarf sprang out in front of him and demanded, 'Where are you going in such haste?'

The young prince paused and answered, 'I'm looking for the Water of Life in order to save my father the King from imminent death.'

'Do you know where to find it?' asked the dwarf.

'Alas, no,' replied the prince with a heavy sigh.

The dwarf's heart softened when he saw the prince's sorrow. How unlike his two older brothers! Here was a prince with a good heart and humility to match!

'Since you have shown me such courtesy, I will tell you where to find it,' he replied. 'You need to go to the enchanted castle where you will find a courtyard and in its centre, a bubbling fountain. You will need to be armed with an iron wand and two loaves of bread in order to succeed. You must knock three times on the castle gate with this wand, and then it will spring open for you. But beware! Inside you will encounter two ferocious lions. Throw each of them a loaf of bread as soon as they open their jaws and they will be as gentle as lambs! Then you must go swiftly and fetch some of the Water of Life before the clock strikes twelve, otherwise the gates will slam shut behind you and there will be no means of escape.'

The prince gratefully accepted the wand and the two loaves of bread from the dwarf and bade him farewell.

He continued until he reached the enchanted castle where everything happened just as the dwarf had told

him. He struck the great gate three times with the wand
and it sprang back to let him enter the courtyard where
two majestic lions basked sleepily in the sun. However,
when they saw the prince they started to drool with
hunger. Quickly, the prince threw them each a loaf of
bread to placate them.

He then strolled through the castle until he came to a great hall where many princes sat as if spellbound at a great banqueting table, staring into the distance, their goblets full, the feast untouched. As he walked amongst them, he removed the jewelled rings from their fingers and grabbed a loaf of bread and a gleaming sword.

The prince then walked through various splendid rooms until he encountered a beautiful princess, as still and silent as if made of marble, seated on a golden throne. He went and knelt before her, so entranced was he by both her beauty and her majesty. Suddenly, the princess clapped her hands with joy and sprang to her feet.

'You have set me free!' she cried. 'I have been forced to sit on that throne for years, unable to move from this place. Now the curse is lifted. In return, I offer myself in marriage, so that we might rule my kingdom together, if you agree?'

The prince was only too delighted to accept her gracious proposal, for he had fallen head over heels in love as soon as he laid eyes on her.

'But first you must complete your quest to save your father,' she reminded him. 'When you have fulfilled your promise to him, return to me in a year and we shall be wed.'

She also told him where to find the fountain for the Water of Life. 'But you must make sure you take the water before the clock strikes twelve,' she warned.

But the prince was too exhausted and all he wanted to do was rest. He found a bedchamber and collapsed into a deep sleep. He awoke with a start to find the clock poised at a quarter to midnight and in a panic he ran through the castle, dodging the shadows, until he reached the fountain. He took a cup that happened to be resting on a ledge and filled it to the brim. He then ran like the wind as he heard the first strike of midnight. The prince was just in time. As he flitted through the gate, it slammed shut, catching the back of his heel.

Holding the cup aloft, the prince mounted his horse and began the journey home. On the way he encountered the dwarf once again. The dwarf congratulated him on his success and when he saw the sword and the loaf of bread said, 'You are fortunate! The sword you carry is capable of defeating whole armies and the bread will continuously replenish itself.'

The prince was delighted to hear this. However,

he was still uneasy. 'I can't return home without my brothers. I would never forgive myself,' he confessed. 'They also went looking for the Water of Life and never came back. Would you happen to know of their whereabouts?'

The dwarf laughed. 'They are precisely where they deserve to be!' he replied. 'I cast a spell on the pair of them and trapped them in a rocky gorge as punishment for their arrogance.'

When the prince heard this he was shocked. 'Please, I beg you, show some compassion,' he pleaded with the dwarf. 'Set them free so all three of us can return to our father, the King.' The dwarf was sceptical, but he eventually relented. 'I will do as you ask,' he replied. 'But mark my words, those brothers of yours are not to be trusted!'

The prince was overjoyed to be reunited with his brothers. He then showed them the cup and explained how he had managed to obtain the Water of Life. He described meeting the beautiful princess who he now intended to marry and, with her, rule her vast kingdom. The brothers listened with stony expressions.

The three then rode into a new kingdom, one that was laid waste due to war and famine. The King of this kingdom was full of despair, convinced they would all perish. The youngest prince came forward and offered the King his sword and the loaf of bread. With this sword, the King defeated his enemies and restored peace to his kingdom. He fed his subjects with the ever-replenishing loaf until their hunger was satisfied. The King gave the sword and the loaf back to the prince and the brothers continued on their journey.

The three princes eventually reached the sea where a large ship awaited them. As they set sail for home, the two older brothers crept off in secret to discuss their situation. Both agreed it did not look good for them, returning home empty-handed while their brother would be handsomely rewarded by the King for saving his life.

'We cannot stand by and let this happen,' they agreed. 'Why should we allow him to steal our chance of happiness?'

In the depths of night, they hatched a cunning plan. Creeping softly to the young prince's cabin, they poured the Water of Life into their cup and refilled the youngest prince's cup with sea water. When the brothers disembarked the ship and returned to the palace in triumph, the young prince went to his father and said, 'I have brought you the Water of Life, father dear. Drink it and you will be saved!'

The King, who was now so frail he could barely raise his head from the pillow, greedily drank from the cup pressed to his lips. But no sooner had he finished the water than he became very sick indeed, retching and moaning, his face a pale shade of green.

The two older brothers, who had been eagerly awaiting this moment, stepped forward and accused their sibling of trying to poison the King. Their performance was so convincing, the King believed them.

'Drink this, father,' they begged him. 'This is the true Water of Life!'

It was true. As soon as the King had taken a few sips from the cup he started to feel reinvigorated. Indeed, by the time he had drained it completely, he was completely restored to health. He felt as he had as a young man and was overwhelmed with gratitude to his sons for saving his life.

Triumphant, the older brothers cornered the young
prince outside the bedchamber and taunted him for
his stupidity.

'It was your undoing, telling us you had found the
Water of Life. You made a big mistake not keeping it
quiet. Why wouldn't we steal it from you and take all
the credit? It was the easiest thing in the world. All we
had to do was creep in at dead of night and steal it from
under your nose,' the middle brother mocked. How
they fell about laughing!

'Now all we have to do is return to the enchanted castle in a year's time and claim the princess for ourselves.'

They warned him against trying to expose the truth to the King, threatening, 'Father will never believe your word against ours. If you keep silent, we will let you live. If you betray us, we'll see to it you are sentenced to death.'

The King believed his youngest and dearest son had tried to kill him and he was full of sorrow. With a heavy heart, he called together his cabinet ministers to decide on an appropriate punishment for such treachery. It was agreed the prince should be taken to a secret place and shot.

Soon afterwards, the young prince went hunting stag in the company of the King's huntsman. They galloped deeper and deeper into the dense forest until they came to a beautiful glade. The prince could not help noticing how the huntsman sighed and appeared close to tears. Moved by what he saw, he asked, 'Whatever is the matter, poor man?'

The huntsman looked about him fearfully and whispered, 'I am not allowed to say, but oh, how I wish I could!'

'Please, you can trust me,' replied the prince.
'It cannot be so bad and whatever it is, I forgive you.'

'The King has ordered me to kill you!' blurted the huntsman.

The prince was horrified by this confession, but he did not blame the huntsman. After all, he was only doing his duty to the King. The prince was shocked. It hurt him deeply that his own father should wish to see him dead.

'Dear huntsman,' he began, 'you are a loyal subject and I do not blame you for carrying out my father's orders. However, I have a proposition for you. If you let me live, I will give you these fine clothes in return for your plainer ones.'

The huntsman was only too relieved to be excused of his duties. He was, after all, very fond of the youngest prince and did not wish to kill him. Happily, the two exchanged their garments and went their separate ways, the huntsman returning home whilst the prince headed deeper into the forest.

Meanwhile, in his absence, three huge wagons laden with gold, silver and precious jewels arrived at the palace. They had been sent by the King who the youngest prince had helped – gifts to thank the prince for helping him overcome the war and famine in his kingdom. After all, he had slain his enemies with the use of the enchanted sword and fed his people with the magic bread. When the prince's father heard this, he was perplexed. He now began to wonder if perhaps his son was honourable after all.

'How I regret having him put to death,' he confided to his courtiers. 'My grief knows no bounds!' Indeed the King was inconsolable, so great was his sorrow. 'Perhaps he was innocent all along!' he wailed.

At this, the huntsman stepped forward, saying, 'Your Majesty, I have something to tell you which may ease your suffering ... I could not bring myself to shoot your son after all.'

He explained to the King how he decided his love for the boy outweighed his duty to the King. 'Thank heavens!' the King cried, clasping the huntsman by the hand in a rare expression of gratitude. Ecstatic at this sudden reversal of fortune, the King immediately issued a royal pardon for the prince and made known far and wide that he had forgiven his son and longed only for his swift return.

Meanwhile, the princess in the enchanted castle had been making preparations for the return of her prince and the wedding. She ordered a road to be built out of pure gold to lead up to the main entrance of the castle.

'Only allow the prince who rides along the centre of this road to enter the castle,' she decreed. 'He alone is the right one. Those who choose to follow other paths are imposters.'

When the year had almost passed and it was time to go and claim the hand of the princess, the oldest prince fancied his chances. Saddling up his horse, he cantered off to the enchanted castle. But when he reached the glittering path of gold, he lost his nerve. 'Better not to ride on such a precious surface,' he told himself, as he swerved to the left and rode alongside all the way to the castle gate. However, when he arrived at the drawbridge, the guards refused him entry, even though he beat his fists against the great oak door.

Soon after, the second brother decided to try his luck with the princess and galloped towards the castle. When he saw the road of gold, he too was dazzled by it and decided to veer his horse to the right in case he damaged its surface. The guards, who had watched him approach, again refused to open the gate and he too was rebuffed and sent away with a flea in his ear.

When the year was at an end, the third son, who had been hiding deep in the heart of the forest, decided to ride to the enchanted castle and honour his pledge to the princess.

Throughout his time in the wilderness, he had never ceased to think about her and how he loved her. He hoped their union might lessen the weight of his sorrows. Indeed, he was so lost in these thoughts as he rode towards the castle, he was oblivious to the fact he was riding along a road made of burnished gold.

When the prince reached the castle, the gate swung back, as if expecting him. Dismounting from his horse, he strode into the great hall, which was festooned with flowers and heady with the scent of lilies. At the far end, stood the princess, resplendent in a white and gold silk dress, a wreath of apple blossom about her head.

Smiling, she held out her hands to him and he ran to meet her. She declared him her rightful bridegroom and sovereign of the realm and they celebrated their wedding that day with great happiness. The only stain on the prince's happiness was his sadness at being estranged from his father at such an important moment in his life.

Later, the princess took him aside and explained to her new husband how she had just received a message from his father the King, expressing his heartfelt remorse and issuing a royal pardon. This completed the prince's happiness. Delighted, the prince, accompanied by his lovely bride, returned to his father who welcomed him with joy. He then felt it was time to tell the King of the treachery of his two older brothers and how he had been silenced by them on pain of death.

When the King heard this, he frowned. Now all he could think of was how he intended to punish them severely. He ordered their arrest, but they had already left the kingdom, rightly fearing their father's anger. But the young prince was not one bent on vengeance and dissuaded his father from pursuing them.

'Let us just be thankful order is restored,' he said. 'You have your health and I have my happiness,' he told him, gazing at his father and his beautiful wife.

The King then smiled at his beloved son. And it was as if the sun had emerged from behind a cloud. 'You are right,' he said. 'All is now well with the world. Let us be content with that!'

They all lived in happiness for the rest of their years and the brothers were never seen or heard from again.

The Three Sisters

There was once an extremely rich king who owned a vast kingdom filled with splendid palaces and castles. He wanted for nothing, and believed his wealth would last forever. He spent his days playing with silver dice on a board crafted out of the finest gold.

But piece by piece, he squandered his entire fortune, selling off his properties to pay for his extravagant habits. Eventually things were so bad, he was forced to move with the Queen and their three daughters to the last remaining castle deep in the darkest depths of a forest. Now their lives were extremely hard and they survived on a diet of potatoes. Life was miserable indeed!

One day the King decided to try his luck at hunting. He filled his pockets with potatoes and strolled into the heart of the forest. But he was not afraid, despite the terrible tales of wild animals: man-eating bears, lions with vicious claws, eagles with razor-sharp beaks that could peck out your eyes, ravenous wolves, all waiting to pounce. Happily he wandered amidst the mighty oaks, oblivious to any danger. Eventually he grew hungry and sat down upon one of the giant tree roots. The King had just begun to eat the potatoes he had stored in his pockets when all of a sudden there was a loud cracking of branches and a giant bear lunged out of the forest with a great roar.

'How dare you sit under my honey tree!' he thundered.

The King, who was now terrified, dropped his potatoes and tried to climb the nearest tree. But before he could even grab hold of a branch, the bear had placed one monstrous paw on his chest and pinned him to the ground.

'Take these potatoes,' cried the King. 'But please don't kill me.'

The bear, who had intended to devour the King (although he was a rather skinny specimen) in two juicy mouthfuls, paused to consider.

Then he rose up on his hind legs and growled:

'How dare you disturb the kingdom of the wild!

As punishment you shall give me your firstborn child!'

The King, cowering, asked in a shaky voice as small as a mouse, 'And what if I refuse? Will you kill me?'

'I had indeed planned to eat you,' the bear reflected. 'But on second thoughts, we could strike a bargain. You can save your own skin if you agree to what I ask. Give me your oldest daughter in marriage. In return, I'll spare your life and give you one hundred sacks of gold.'

The King, who felt he was in no position to disagree (the weight of the bear's paw had snuffed all the breath out of him), was only too ready to agree to the bear's proposition. After all, what else could he do?

'I will give her to you,' he sighed, 'as long as you let me go in peace.'

The bear removed his paw and led the King out of the forest.

'Just remember,' he growled, 'in a week's time I will return to claim my bride.'

But the King had no intention of keeping his part of the pact now he was a free man. The idea of it! Sending his oldest daughter to live with a wild bear ... it was unthinkable! So he barred the entrance to his castle and ordered all the gates to be locked. He told his oldest daughter not to worry, he had no intention of honouring the pact he had made with the bear. However, erring on the side of caution, he concealed the princess in a turret high up in the castle and told her to stay there until the week was at an end.

But when the seventh day dawned in all its glory, a splendid coach drew up at the castle entrance, pulled by six fine horses. It was escorted by many knights attired in all their glittering finery and armour. Simultaneously, the front gate of the castle fell open, and all the keys sprang from their locks as the carriage pulled up in the main courtyard.

67

The King, hearing all the commotion of horses and hooves, went to see what had caused it. As he stuck his head out of a turret window, he was just in time to spy his eldest daughter being helped into the carriage by a handsome prince.

All he could do was lean out and call after her:

'Darling daughter so dear to me,

How I wish I could set you free!

Farewell, my daughter dear.

I see you are off to wed the bear!'

The princess forlornly waved her handkerchief from the carriage window as it flew away at great speed, as if harnessed to the wind, and disappeared deep into the enchanted forest.

The Queen was beside herself with grief when she learned of her eldest daughter's fate. She cried as if her heart would break. The King wept bitter tears, too. He felt very guilty indeed about the bargain he had struck with the bear. But what could he have done differently? Weeping would change nothing. On the fourth day after the princess's disappearance, the King ventured down to the courtyard where he found a large wooden chest made of finest oak. When the King opened it, he was dazzled by its contents. It contained the hundred bags of gold promised to him by the bear.

The gold proved to be some consolation for his loss. After all, the King did not have much inclination to question his conscience. He soon returned to his former life of luxury, moving from palace to palace, playing at dice and frittering away his money at every opportunity.

It was not long before he had to sell all his property and move back to his castle in the forest. Again, he reverted to a diet of potatoes and foraging for food in the woods. He had a falcon, and one day he took it on his arm and went out to the meadow to see if it might spy some prey. However, as soon as he released the bird, it flew off towards the enchanted forest. The King watched as the falcon soared then swooped down into the darkness of the forest.

A moment later, the falcon reappeared in a flurry of feathers, chased by an eagle. The eagle's vast shadow blotted out the sun as its wings beat the air and it closed in on the smaller bird. The falcon returned to the King who tried to ward off the eagle by jabbing at it with his spear. But the larger bird merely caught the falcon in its talons and crushed it in one swift movement. He then dug his claws deep into the King's shoulder and said:

'How dare you disturb the kingdom of the wild!
As punishment you shall give me your second child!'

The King, seeing the eagle's razor-sharp beak, fell to his knees in submission. 'My second daughter is yours for the taking,' he replied. 'But what will you give me in return?'

'Two hundred bags of gold,' replied the eagle. 'I shall come for your daughter in seven weeks.'

The eagle then released the quivering King from his vice-like grip and flew back into the enchanted forest. The King returned to his palace and did not mention to a soul the bargain he had been forced to strike with the eagle.

The weeks passed peacefully enough. But on the last day of the seventh week, the princess was reclining reading a book on the lawn of the castle when a procession of knights arrived on horseback. At its helm was the most striking knight of all, who leaped down from his stallion and declared:

'Come up here,
Princess dear
And wed this eagle
Without fear!'

Without waiting for her answer, the knight took her in his broad feathered arms and flew away with her to the magic forest. The King and Queen were in a state of shock, half expecting the princess to reappear at any moment in the weeks that followed. But she did not. It was then the King admitted to his wife he had saved his own life by promising the eagle his daughter in return.

No words could describe the Queen's grief at losing another child. The King suffered too, although his grief was lessened soon afterwards when he discovered two giant eggs, each weighing a hundred bags of gold, sitting on the lawn. The eagle had honoured his side of the bargain. The eggs shone in all their goldness and the King said to himself, 'Money is a sign of faith after all.'

Once again, the King resumed his extravagant lifestyle, spending as if there were no tomorrow. It was not long before he had run out of money and was forced to return to the castle in the forest.

It was left to his youngest daughter, the last of the princesses, to boil the potatoes that fed the three of them. The King had lost his desire to hunt for hares in the forest and birds in the sky. Instead, he rather fancied living on a diet of fish, so his poor daughter wove him a net with her bare hands.

The King took the net with him to the sea's edge, beyond the forest, where a small boat rested on its sandy shore. He then rowed out into the middle of a deep blue lagoon and cast his net over the side.

It was not long before he felt a tug. When he pulled in the net he found it alive and squirming with silver-speckled flounders. However, when he dipped his oars in the water and started to row for the shore, the boat was stuck fast to the spot. As hard as he tried, it would not budge.

Suddenly, the sea swelled and a giant whale broke its surface, nearly swallowing the boat whole.

'Who gave you permission to catch and kill the subjects of my realm?' the whale boomed, its mouth as wide and dark as a cave.

The King was petrified as he gazed in horror at those wide jaws and his courage failed him for a third time. It was then he remembered his youngest child.

'Spare my life,' he shouted as the boat rocked wildly, 'and I will give you my youngest daughter!'

The whale thrashed his tail from side to side causing huge black waves as he reflected on the King's offer.

'I agree to your terms,' he eventually roared. 'I will also give you something of value in return for the princess. I do not possess any gold or silver. However, the seabed is strewn with priceless pearls and these I will give you in sackloads. I will come for my bride at the end of the seventh month.' With one giant flick of his tail, the whale disappeared beneath the surface.

The King rowed back to the shore with his catch and returned to the castle. His last daughter baked the fish he had caught. But when they were placed before him on the table, the King no longer had the stomach to eat them. In truth, he felt sick with himself for having been so weak in the face of danger. Gazing at his last and most precious daughter, he felt as if a thousand knives were cutting through him, so great was his remorse.

For months afterwards, his wife and the princess noted how the King did not smile once. Nor did he tell the Queen of his folly. As the months passed, he allowed himself to hope perhaps this time his fears were false and she would be spared.

One day, at the end of the seventh month, the princess went into the courtyard to draw some water from the well. As she raised the bucket, a carriage pulled by six fine horses and footmen attired in silver thundered across the drawbridge and pulled up in front of her. When the carriage door opened, out stepped the handsomest prince she had ever laid eyes on. He asked her for a glass of water and when she gave it to him, he took her in his arms and lifted her into the coach. Then they were off in a cloud of dust, cantering towards the blue sea. As the road transformed into a river, the Queen happened to glance out of her window and her eyes alighted on something that defied belief. She saw her daughter, in all her wedding finery, riding upon a whale's back as the river ran towards the vast blue sea. Throwing open the window, the Queen leaned out as far as she dared and cried after her:

'Farewell my daughter dear.

Gone to wed the whale I fear!'

The Queen still searched high and low for her daughter, unable to believe she had truly vanished. Surely it was some terrible mistake. But her cries echoed around the empty castle. Then there was silence. It was at that moment that the Queen broke down and wept as if she would never stop.

The King, seeing her grief, crumbled and confessed his sordid part in agreeing to all his daughters being married against their will in exchange for the beasts sparing his life. (He did, however, neglect to mention the gold for fear of causing her further distress.) The King explained the whale had come to claim their daughter as a result of his foolish bargain. He admitted this had been the reason for his sadness all these months, knowing she would be taken from them. But there was some comfort. They would be rich again, if the whale had indeed kept his promise. However, the Queen would not be comforted. Did he not understand their youngest daughter was beyond any value?

'How could all the pearls in the ocean replace my darling daughter?' she cried.

The Queen remained inconsolable for a long time afterwards. Then one day she discovered, to her great surprise, she was pregnant again. Since this child was an unexpected gift, they decided to call him Reinald the Wonder Child.

His birth brought the King and Queen great solace. He grew into a fine strong boy and the Queen often told him about the three sisters he had never known, and how they were all held captive by wild beasts in the enchanted forest. The boy listened carefully to the sad history of the three princesses and was filled with indignation at their terrible fate. As soon as he turned sixteen, he demanded a set of armour and sword from the King and with his parents' blessing, set out to avenge his sisters.

Straight as an arrow, he headed for the forest, determined to find the princesses and slay the beasts. He spent some days wandering in the wilderness without encountering a single living thing, until he came upon the strangest scene. In a clearing there sat a young woman, a small bear cub resting his soft furry head in her lap, whilst around them two young cubs gamboled and played at her feet. Reinald immediately surmised she must be his oldest sister and these three cubs, her children.

Stepping out of the gloom of the forest he said, 'Dearest sister, I am your brother Reinald and I have come to find you.'

The princess nearly jumped out of her skin when she
looked up and saw another human being. And yet she
immediately saw how closely he resembled her father
the King. But her joy was eclipsed by fear when she
realized he was telling the truth.

'Dearest brother,' she whispered, suddenly white
with terror. 'You must not linger here, for if my
husband, the bear, discovers you here, he will kill you
without mercy!'

But Reinald was not easily afraid. 'Dear sister,' he replied, 'I have found you and I have no intention of leaving you now I have found you. Please tell me your story.'

When she saw her brother was deadly earnest, she quickly took him to a large cave on the side of a mountain, concealed amongst the pine trees. Reinald realized, with horror, this was where the princess lived with the bear and his cubs. On one side of the cave was a pile of straw and dead leaves where the bears slept, whilst opposite was a magnificent four-poster bed for the princess, covered in red velvet trimmed with gold.

'You must hide!' she warned Reinald, pushing him under the bed.

No sooner had she hidden her brother, than a giant shadow loomed in the mouth of the cave. The bear had returned to his lair.

'I smell, I smell the flesh of a human being,' he growled, raising himself up on his hind legs and sniffing the air. He made to paw under the bed, but the princess stepped in front of him and said, 'Calm down! Who on earth would want to come here?'

But the bear was not so easily thrown off the scent. 'I came across a horse in the forest and devoured it in a couple of mouthfuls. I know where there's a horse, there's also a man!'

He ambled back to the bed. 'I smell something,' he whined, pawing at the velvet cover to see beneath. But the princess ran over to him and started stroking him behind the ears.

'You are mistaken, dearest,' she said. 'Why don't you rest until dinner is ready?'

The bear growled and grumbled as he reluctantly stooped down and allowed the princess to tickle him behind his ears. Suddenly docile, he put one paw in his mouth, flopped down on the straw and fell into a deep sleep.

The princess then crawled under the bed next to her brother to relate her story. She described how every seven days the bear was restored to his natural form. He would be transformed into a handsome prince, his cave a magnificent castle, and the animals in the forest his servants. It was on such a day that he had come to claim her for his wife. She had returned with him to his castle where she was greeted by a dazzling array of courtiers. A magnificent celebration took place that evening and after the festivities, she went with her bridegroom to their splendid bedchamber. However, when she awoke the next morning, she found herself in this cave in the company of a wild bear growling at her feet. Her four-poster bed and the items she had laid her hands on were the only items that remained unaltered. The six days that followed were a torture. But on the seventh day, everything reverted to how it was when she first met the prince.

The princess did not grow old because only that one day each week counted in her life, so she was relatively happy with her existence. In time, she gave the bear three sons, who, like their father, became human for one day each week. She gathered together an assortment of delicious cakes, fruit and meats and hid them in the straw so her family might live off these supplies during the week. In return, the bear obeyed his wife and did as she commanded.

When Reinald woke from his slumbers, he found himself lain between silk sheets in a luxurious bed. Servants then arrived to dress him in fine robes. Then his sister entered, accompanied by her three handsome boys and her husband, the bear prince. They were all overjoyed to see one another and spent the day celebrating in the magnificent surroundings of the palace. All too soon, the sun sank low in the flaming sky and the princess was filled with sadness.

'My dear brother, it is time for you to leave us,' she said. 'For if you are still here at dawn, my husband will not be able to control his natural instincts and he will eat you.'

The bear prince handed Reinald three long bear hairs.

'Keep these,' he told him. 'If ever you are in danger, just rub these hairs together and I will come to your aid.'

Then they embraced and Reinald drove away in carriage drawn by six horses. He travelled a great distance through forests and deserts, over mountains and through valleys, until the sky began to fade to a deep violet. Then suddenly Reinald found himself thrown to the ground, the fine horses and carriage disappeared.

When daylight came and he looked about him, he spied six ants scuttling off, pulling a walnut behind them. Reinald realized he was still in the enchanted forest, so he decided to search for his second sister.

Again, the first three days yielded no clues as to her whereabouts. But on the fourth day, he caught sight of a great eagle as it swooped down and landed on its nest in a great linden tree.

Concealing himself nearby, he waited until it took to the skies again, beating the air with giant

wings. Then Reinald ran to the foot of the tree
and shouted up at the nest, 'Dearest sister, it is me,
Reinald, your brother come to find you! Are you
up there?'

'If you are indeed my brother, come up and see me,
Reinald!' came her reply.

But as hard as he tried, Reinald could not get a grip
on the vast trunk of the linden tree. Suddenly, a ladder
woven out of silk dropped down and he clambered
up until he reached the nest that was intricately
constructed out of velvety moss and twigs. Amidst the
foliage, beneath a canopy of rose-coloured silk, sat his
sister, a large egg resting in her lap.

'I am keeping it warm until it is ready to hatch,' she
explained as they embraced, overjoyed to meet for the
first time.

But suddenly the princess's eyes clouded and she
pulled him close and whispered. 'Dear brother, you
must not stay here, for if my eagle husband spies you
with his eagle eye, he will pluck out your eyes and
peck out your heart! Indeed, he has already killed
three of the servants who were accompanying you on
your journey.'

'I have no intention of deserting you,' replied her brother. 'I will wait for your eagle husband to transform himself into a prince once again, and then perhaps I can reason with him.'

The princess showed Reinald a hollow in the base of the mighty linden tree where he might secrete himself, and each day she lowered food from her eyrie so her brother did not starve in his hiding place. Whenever the eagle was absent from the nest, Reinald would climb up to while away the hours with his beautiful sister.

After six weeks of waiting, it happened – the eagle was transformed into a prince. Reinald woke in a splendid chamber and there were great celebrations as the prince and the brother and sister became acquainted. However, on the seventh evening they were forced to bid their farewells. The eagle prince gave Reinald three feathers and said, 'If ever you need me, rub them together and I will come at once.'

The eagle prince gave his servants to escort the prince on his journey. But when dawn rekindled in the east, Reinald found he was alone, stood on a rugged high cliff looking out across the vast ocean that glittered like knives in the morning sun.

His thoughts turned to his third sister. Perhaps
he might find her there. For three days he struggled
through a dense wilderness down to the coast, and
when he stood at last on the pale moon crescent of sand
fringing the sea, he called:

'Dearest sister, if you are in the sea,

It's your brother, Reinald, come to set you free!'

But only the sea's roar answered him, so he threw
some crumbs of bread to a red-speckled flounder,
saying, 'Go tell her Reinald the Wonder Child is here!'

But the flounder merely devoured the bread and
swam away. Then he spied a small rowing boat pushed
up against the shore, so he jumped aboard and began
to row, until he saw a chimney made of salt crystal
protruding from the sea.

A wonderful aroma floated across the water,
convincing him this was her dwelling place. Tethering
his boat, Reinald climbed inside the chimney's spout
and slid down into an underwater cavern where the
princess was waiting. But her joy at seeing Reinald was
tempered by fear.

'My husband the whale has got wind of your visit,'
she confided. 'He will not be able to control his desire
to swallow you whole if he finds you here, and he will
destroy this fragile cavern
with one swish of his
tail and I will
surely drown!'

'Then conceal me somewhere,' Reinald replied.

'How can I?' replied his sister helplessly. 'The crystal walls are transparent, can't you see?'

But then she remembered the wood pile in one of the antechambers and hid Reinald in its midst.

Then the whale came, its black shadow surging past the thin skin of crystal that separated the princess from the sea. Once, he caught a glimpse of Reinald's jacket sticking out of the wood pile and started wildly thrashing the sea with his tail. The princess trembled like an aspen leaf until he swam away. The whale besieged the crystal palace for some weeks, circling its walls, hoping to catch another glimpse of the intruder.

But one morning, Reinald awoke to find himself in a splendid castle on an island, a castle that far surpassed those of the bear and the eagle princes in its grandeur. For a month he lived with his sister and the whale prince. When it came to an end, the prince handed him three scales and said, 'If you ever need my help, just rub these three scales together and I will come to you.'

The whale prince took Reinald back to the shore where his sword and armour lay on the sand. There was genuine sadness at their parting, because the whale prince and Reinald had become firm friends. It would have been easier to stay, it was true. But Reinald knew his duty was ultimately to save his sisters and restore their freedom. He had promised his parents and he was an honourable young man.

Therefore, Reinald the Wonder Child took up his sword and embarked on a journey for seven days and seven nights, into the wildest country imaginable, sleeping under a vast velvet canopy of twinkling stars. Eventually, he came to a dark and forbidding castle that loomed over the landscape.

The sight of it struck fear into his heart, but Reinald did not flinch as he rode over the drawbridge. However, his heart missed a beat when he saw how the steel gate was guarded by a monstrous black bull, the muscles rippling beneath its tough hide, its eyes flaming with rage. As it charged at Reinald, he drew his sword and dealt a powerful blow to the bull's thick neck.

However, imagine his surprise as the sword merely snapped, as if glass had smote steel! Snorting fiercely, the bull turned and charged again, tossing Reinald high into the air. It was in his moment of desperation, Reinald remembered the three bear hairs. In a split second, he pulled them from his pocket and rubbed them together.

Suddenly, the bear appeared out of nowhere and lumbered between the bull and Reinald, shielding him from the monster. He knew at that moment the beast had come to protect him! Raising himself up on his hind legs, the bear gave a mighty bellow before lunging at the bull and tearing it apart with his claws.

But Reinald's ordeal was not over yet. Suddenly, he saw a small bird burst in a flurry of feathers from the ripped stomach of the bull and take flight. Instinctively, he reached into his pocket and rubbed the three feathers together.

Out of the blue, an eagle swooped down and plucked the bird from the sky, piercing it in the neck with its razor-sharp beak. Falling away from the sun, the eagle then shook the bird senseless and cast it aside as if it were a rag doll. But as it plummeted earthwards, to Reinald's astonishment, the bird laid a golden egg. Gleaming in the sunlight, it dropped like a stone and disappeared into a fast-flowing river.

Reinald, wary of this being yet another cunning trick designed to outwit him, reached in his pocket for a third time and rubbed the three fish scales together.

A silvery salmon popped its head out of the water, then swam down to the muddy riverbed and swallowed the egg before darting up to the surface. Leaping from the water in a clear arc, the fish spat out the golden egg at Reinald's feet.

Overcome by curiosity, he found a sharp stone and cracked it open. Imagine his astonishment when, on feeling inside the egg's cavity, he discovered a key.

As soon as Reinald touched the gate's lock with the key, all the doors and windows of the castle sprang open. The young prince began to walk, as if in a dream, passing through seven doors, one after the other. Each door led into a magnificent room, each one more splendid than the last, furnished with fine tapestries and dripping with chandeliers.

Finally, Reinald passed into the seventh and most lavishly furnished room, with an oak four-poster bed decked in crimson silk. A beautiful princess lay in a deep sleep upon its velvet cover, long waves of auburn hair framing her heart-shaped face.

Reinald stood, gazing down at her, so dazzled was he by her beauty. He tried to wake her, gently at first. Reinald touched her hands, cool as alabaster, but still but she did not stir. He spoke tender words of love in her ear. Nothing! In desperation he drew his sword from its jewelled scabbard and struck the slab of slate that lay next to her bed. There was a terrible cracking and splintering. For an instant she was roused from her slumber, her emerald eyes flashing briefly as she tried to focus them on Reinald, only to shut them fast again, the desire to sleep too great to resist. Would nothing induce her to awaken?

Exasperated, the prince picked up the slate and dashed it on the ground. The slate splintered into a thousand pieces and at last the princess opened her eyes and slipped from her bed, her pale complexion blooming like a rose when she saw the fine prince stood before her.

'How can I ever thank you?' she addressed him, her voice the sweetest music.

She revealed herself as the sister of Reinald's three brothers-in-law. She had rejected the advances of an evil sorcerer who had then cast a spell on her and her poor brothers, condemning her to a death-like sleep and changing her brothers into wild creatures. Only the destruction of the magic slate could free them from the sorcerer's curse.

'Now you have set me free!' she told him, radiant with happiness, as they explored the castle together and became better acquainted.

Now there was great cause for celebration. When Reinald and the princess eventually emerged from the castle, they saw the three princes and their families riding to meet them. Finally, the princes had been released from the curse. The eagle princess held a baby in her arms hatched from the magic egg she had so lovingly nurtured.

Triumphant, Reinald the Wonder Child and his three sisters returned to the King and Queen who were now grown old. Their joy was complete. The King had learned a harsh lesson. Kneeling before his wife and children, he asked for their forgiveness.

His life had been empty and deprived of meaning without his children by his side, and he had lived to regret his terrible folly. The King now realized that all the riches of the world were no compensation for the loss of those you love. Indeed, for the rest of his days, there was nothing more precious to him than his family.